The ADVENTURES TOMMY AND TINA

Dreaming Of Being A Termite
And Finding A Home In The Forest

To order additional copies of this book, contact:
Xlibris
844-714-8691
www.Xlibris.com
Orders@Xlibris.com

ISBN: Softcover   978-1-6641-4803-1
       EBook   978-1-6641-4802-4

Print information available on the last page

Rev. date: 02/23/2021

This book is dedicated to my grandchildren,
Kyle, Hannah, Erin, Sydney, Maddie and Ryan.

An Educational story for young children that will improve and build relationships and communications with their older family members.

ROD BURNS

The Adventures TOMMY and TINA

Tommy and Tina childhood friends were walking thru the forest near their home carrying their picnic lunch and saw a lot of bugs flying from an old rotten log laying on the ground, tommy said, I think those are termites, wow said Tina, I wonder where they are going? After lunch Tommy and Tina started dreaming about where the termites were flying too.

The Story of Tommy and Tina Termite

It was late spring, the flowers were in bloom and the leaves on the trees were shading the forest floor, the grumbling of thunder could be heard in the distance as the dark fluffy clouds rolled across the sky. The heat of the afternoon and the moisture from the approaching rain made it the perfect time for Tina and Tommy Termite to say goodbye to their family colony of termites and begin their journey to find a new home and start their own new colony. Saying goodbye was hard because they had so many good friends in the colony but they knew it was time to find their new home. Tommy and Tina had planned for some time for this day to come, because they could see the colony of termites getting very large and needing more room for the baby termites. Tommy and Tina were young adult termites and ready to start their own family.

As Tommy and Tina Flew away from their home in the old stump they waved good bye to their old friends and family. Their friends shouted Goodbye, Goodbye, Goodbye Tommy and Tina. As Tommy and Tina were flying away, Tina said to Tommy, I was glad to leave that old stump; it was getting very crowded in there. It feels good to be out on our own. Let's go and look for a home of our own in the forest.

Tina says to Tommy, what a beautiful morning, look there is Sherry the Squirrel eating some acorns, lets fly over and ask her were she lives. Hi Sherry the Squirrel, what are you doing asked Tommy and Tina? I am cracking acorns that have fallen from the tree, so I can eat the nuts inside. Crack, crack went Sherry the squirrel, as she broke the shell of the acorn and chew, chew, chew as she ate the nut inside. We are looking for a new home said Tommy and Tina, where do you live Sherry the squirrel?

Sherry waving her fuzzy long tail went crack, crack and then set down her acorn and said, "I live at the top of the tree in the round nest made of leaves and twigs and grass". I can see all over the forest from my house. Tommy and Tina said, that must be a wonderful view but that's too high in the sky for us to live. We need to find a home close to the ground. Goodbye Sherry, Goodbye, Goodbye, Sherry went back to cracking her acorn. Crack, Crack, Crack. Good meeting you Sherry the squirrel, we will stop by again sometime.

Tommy and Tina flew off into the forest.

Look, says Tommy, there is Freddy the fox. Let's ask him where he lives. Hello says Tommy and Tina, how are you today Freddy the fox. (In a deep voice) Freddy said, "I am doing fine". What, are you doing Freddy the fox, said Tina. Freddy said, I am building my new home deep in this rock pile for my family. We are calling it our den. Dick and Ann are our new babies so we needed a larger home. The den in the rocks looks like a nice safe place to live for your family says Tommy, I wish we could live in the rocks, but we need to be near moist wood that we can eat, rocks are very hard to chew said Tommy, What do you eat Freddy, said Tina. I eat small rodents said Freddy the fox. Wow, said Tina that would give me a belly ache. There are plenty of dead moist trees in the forest, said Freddy. Thank you for the information said Tommy. Let's get on our way, Goodbye Freddy yelled Tommy and Tina, Freddy yelled, good luck finding your new home, goodbye, Tommy and Tina yelled Freddy the fox and his babies Ann and Dick as they flew away.

Robin and Ryan the red breast flew by and said, Hey Tommy and Tina stop by our nest for a visit, chirped Robin the red breast, we will said Tina. So Tommy and Tina Termite flew up to the tree limb where Robin and Ryan the red breast was sitting on a limb next to her home in the oak tree. Say hi, to my new babies said Robin the red breast; their names are Joe, Skip, and Marie. Chirp, Chirp, Chirp Hello said the babies.

Hello said Tommy and Tina. What are you eating said Tommy, Worms said Robin the Red breast. We eat moist wood says Tina and we are looking for a place to build our new home. There is plenty of wood in the forest, said Ryan the red breast; you will find a nice place to live here in the forest. Goodbye, Goodbye, Goodbye as Tommy and Tina waved as they flew away. Chirp, chirp, chirp went Joe, Skip and Marie the baby red breast.

As Tommy and Tina flew away Tina said to Tommy, I bet worms are very wiggly in your mouth to swallow.

Look Tina said Tommy, there is Ollie the owl, let's go over and talk to Ollie. Hi Ollie the Owl said Tommy and Tina. Hoot, hoot said Ollie the owl. Ollie, have you seen any moist logs or old tree stumps around here, we are looking for a nice place to build our new home. Ollie said no, I only go out at night and Hoot at the moon. Where do you live Ollie the owl? Ollie said I live in that tree with the hole in it. That looks like a nice home said Tommy. Where do you go to eat dinner said Tina, I fly in the forest and look for mice said Ollie. Well it has been good talking to you Ollie we need to be on our way to find a new home. See you soon Ollie, said Tommy and Tina. As Tommy and Tina were flying away they said to each other, let's find a home far from where Ollie the owl lives, I think he would keep us from going to sleep with all that hooting he does at night, your right said Tina, besides his breath smells a little funny.

Look says Tommy there is Sharon the Skunk, Let's not talk to her said Tina, she stinks and her home smells funny too. Tommy said she only stinks when she sprays at you and only when she does not like you. How do you know she will like us said Tina? Tommy said you are right, let's talk to Sharon the Skunk another time.

Look Tina says Tommy there is Woody the Wood Pecker, let's go and talk to him, he knows a lot about wood. Hi Woody said Tommy and Tina, Peck, Peck, Peck, Peck went Woody the Wood pecker. What are you eating said Tina. Some nasty insects and bugs that live on trees, said Woody. I am just cleaning up around my home said Woody, would you like to come into my tree for a visit. Thanks said Tommy and Tina but we need to be on our way to finding a new home. Good bye Woody, said Tommy. Peck, peck, peck said Woody, good bye. Tina said to Tommy as they flew away in a hurry, I am glad Woody did not think we were bugs. He might have eaten us for dinner said Tommy, Wow that was a close call said Tina. I did not like the way Woody looked at us said, Tina, let's find a home far away from Woody.

Tommy said to Tina, let's look for Chucky the Chip monk he knows his way around the forest, maybe he can show us some nice places to live. Look there is Chucky the chip monk next to the large log, Hey Chucky said Tommy and Tina termite. Is this your home? Yes said Chucky the chip monk, I live in this fallen log and there are plenty of greens for me to eat, it is a nice place to live. Are there any other fallen trees or tree stumps around here ask Tina, Oh yes said Chucky fly over towards the stream and you will find plenty of places to live, thanks Chucky we will see you later.

Look Tina over in the high ferns, it is Debbie the deer with her new baby fawn. Hi Debbie the deer said Tina, is that your new baby, yes said Debbie the deer, she is only a few weeks old, her name is Maddie, we just finished taking a nap in these cool ferns and now it is time to go and eat some flowers and green bushes. How far to the stream, said Tina, just over the hill said Debbie the deer. We are looking for our new home, said Tina, see you soon Debbie.

Let's fly up the hill Tommy said Tina. Is that Mike and Michelle the moose walking up the hill said Tommy, let's fly by and say hello. Look at those big antlers on Michelle the moose said Tommy. Girls do not have antlers, said Tina, only a male moose has antlers. Hey Mike the moose, how are you today, (in a deep voice) just fine said Mike. How do you keep your antlers so sharp and shiny Mike, asked Tina. (In a deep voice) I rub my antlers against the trees, said Mike the Moose, it is like scratching my head, and it feels great. We are looking for a new home near the stream, is it close by? Yes said Mike the moose, just over the hill. Good meeting you Mike and Michelle we need to look for a new home said Tina. Tina said to Tommy as they flew away, let's not pick a home that Mike the moose would like to scratch his antlers on, because it would make our home wiggle, good idea Tina said Tommy.

Tommy and Tina are flying through the trees and Tommy says to Tina, look over behind the tree, it is Barbara the black bear scratching her claws on the tree with her new baby bear cub, they must have just come out of their den to look for their dinner, let's not get to close said Tina they have a loud roar and it will hurt our ears. Hey Barbara the bear said Tommy is that your new baby cub, yes said Barbara his name is John. Is that your home over in the side of the hill said Tina, yes said Barbara the bear, we call it our cave. Roar, Roar went John the bear cub; he must be hungry said Barbara. We are going down to the stream to catch some fish for dinner said John. Have a good Dinner said Tommy, we will see you soon said Tina, as Tommy and Tina flew away, Tina said let's live far away from Barbara and John the bear family, their loud roaring would scare me and keep us awake.

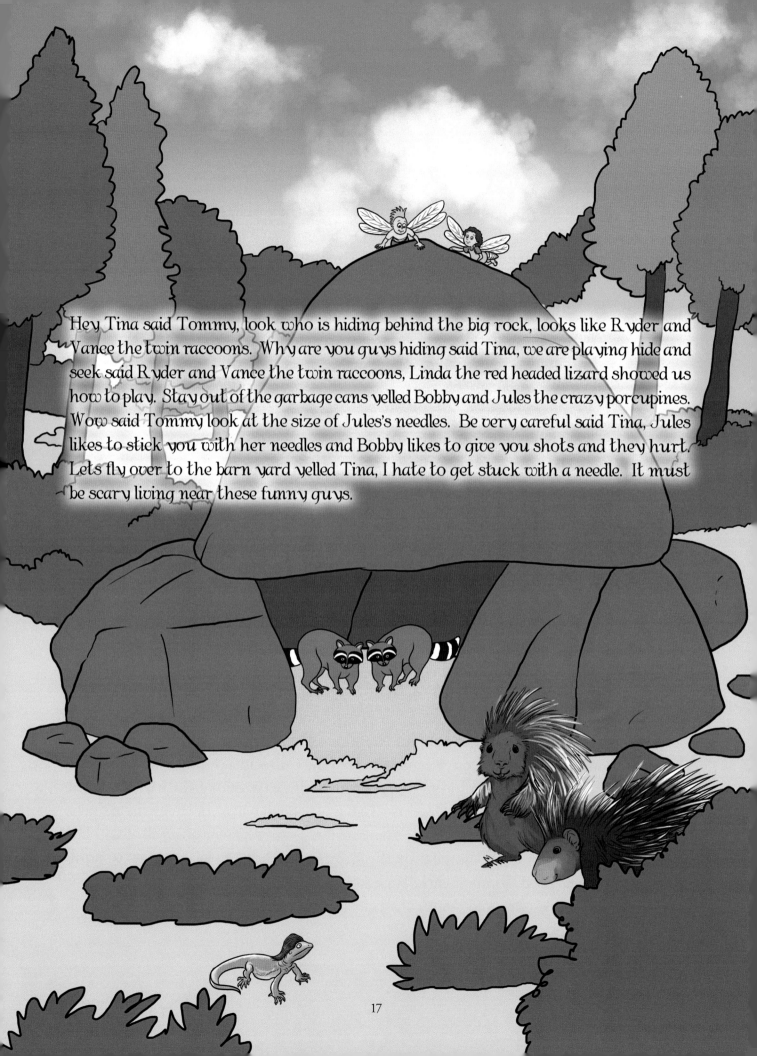

Hey Tina said Tommy, look who is hiding behind the big rock, looks like Ryder and Vance the twin raccoons. Why are you guys hiding said Tina, we are playing hide and seek said Ryder and Vance the twin raccoons, Linda the red headed lizard showed us how to play. Stay out of the garbage cans yelled Bobby and Jules the crazy porcupines. Wow said Tommy look at the size of Jules's needles. Be very careful said Tina, Jules likes to stick you with her needles and Bobby likes to give you shots and they hurt. Lets fly over to the barn yard yelled Tina, I hate to get stuck with a needle. It must be scary living near these funny guys.

Tommy and Tina flying

Look Tina there is a farm over there, maybe the barn is rotten and that might be a good place to live. Barn wood is good to eat said Tommy. What kind of animal is that Tina, said Tommy, that is it a horse, said Tommy, Ha! Ha! Said Tina, that is not a horse, Henry the horse is over in the corral that is Dennis the Donkey, he haw, he haw went Dennis the donkey. Henry the horse can run much faster than Dennis the Donkey. Dennis the donkey looks a little funny but I bet he is fun to ride. They both like to eat fresh hay and corn and live in the barn. Never go behind Henry the horse or Dennis the Donkey because they might kick you and that kick would really hurt said Tina. Speaking of being hurt, there is Bruce the bull, He has big horns and likes to chase Chet the cow, and he is a little scary to be around. Chet the cow eats a lot of grass and hay and each day farmer Bob gets milk from his cows. George the goat gives milk to the farmer too and George eats a lot of grass down to the roots. Hey Tina is that a Kangaroo, what is he doing here, Tommy that is Kent the Kangaroo, he is the pet of Bob the farmer. Bob brought him all the way back from Australia when he was on vacation. That is a little funny to see Kent the Kangaroo in a barn yard.

Look at Penny the pig rolling around in the mud with her piglets. That looks like fun but I wonder how they take a bath. Look there is Hannah the hen carrying her eggs. Hannah the Hen lives in the chicken coop, she keeps a very messy house said Erin the Eagle, Wow said Tina I did not see you flying by Erin the Eagle, where are you flying to said Tina, back to my nest at the top of the mountain said Erin the Eagle. See you soon said Tommy. I will keep an eye open for you Tommy. Bark! Bark! Said Dave the dog, how do you like our farm. It is wonderful said Tommy and Tina. Meet my new puppy Pat, bark, bark said Pat the puppy. Pat the puppy keeps our dog house very clean said Dave the Dog. Where is Kathy the Cat said Tommy, over there said Dave the dog, Kathy the Cat is sneaking up on Sydney the snake, Kathy the cat will never catch Sydney the snake because Sydney the snake lives in the ground and is as quick as Butch the bunny rabbit. Tina said it was sure nice meeting all of you but we need to look for a new home near the steam so we have a place to sleep tonight. See you soon yelled Tommy, bark, bark went Pat the puppy, he, haw went Dennis the donkey, oink, oink said Penny the pig; sissssssss said Sydney the snake, see you soon. Good luck finding a home.

Hey Tommy, said Tina; let's look over by the pond for a new home. Good idea Tina, look there is Linda the lizard, be careful talking to her said Tommy, Lizards have very long tongues and they eat insects and bugs, wow said Tina, let's stay away from that big tongue. Hey there is Kyle the Quacking duck, quack, quack said Kyle. Do not ask Kyle the quacking duck a lot of questions, said Tommy or we will be here all day. Kyle is a talker but knows a lot about the pond and stream. Hey Kyle how is the water? Wet but there is a lot of good fish in here to eat, would you like some dinner? No thanks Kyle said Tommy we only eat wet wood. How does that taste, said Kyle, moist and chewy said Tina. I like my fish said Kyle Quack, Quack. Have you seen any tree stumps or wet logs near the stream Kyle, said Tina. Oh yes there are plenty, said Kyle. Ask, Gretchen the goose she knows a lot about the water. Hey Gretchen the goose, have you seen any fallen logs near the stream said Tommy, oh yes there are plenty said Gretchen. We are on our way over to the stream said Tommy, see you soon, honk, honk said Gretchen.

Hey tommy said Tina, let's fly up and sit with Erin the Eagle high on the mountain, from there we will be able to see the whole stream and we can pick a good place to live, great idea said Tommy. Hey Erin can we sit with you for a while, you have the best spot to see the whole stream and it should be easy to find a good place to live. Erin said, if I were a termite I would follow Becky the beaver up the stream and she will show you a lot of great places to have a home. Thanks Erin, what a good idea, let's go Tommy it is getting dark and we need to find a home before night comes. Hey Becky the beaver, we are looking for a nice place to live. Do you know of any places near the stream where there is a fallen log, oh yes just follow me and my new babies Larry, Cathy, Diane and Norm. How is this log, Tina and Tommy, it is a large log and near a stump in a very shady area, this is perfect Becky, thank you for helping us find a nice place to build our new home, said Tommy and Tina. Look there is Patsy, Richard and Debbie, the frog family welcoming us to our new home. Hey look Tina, it is Rod the raccoon with his friend Sid the sloth telling us they will watch over our new home while we sleep tonight, I guess they are the night police said Tommy. I feel safe now said Tina. I am getting very sleepy Tommy, said Tina, let's eat into our log house and then get a good nights sleep. Good Idea Tina, it has been a long and exciting day. Tommy, do not forget to say your good night prayers, said Tina, we have a lot to be thankful for, Good Night!!!! Sweet Dreams!!!!!!!

Printed in the United States
By Bookmasters